T0164402

Rebozos

Poems by Carmen Tafolla

Paintings by Catalina Gárate García

With an historical afterword by
  Hector García Manzanedo, Ph.D.

Rebozos

WingsPress

San Antonio, Tejas
2012

Rebozos © 2012 by Wings Press for Carmen Tafolla and Catalina Gárate García

All artwork is by Catalina Gárate García and is used by permission of the artist.

Designed by Thelma Muraida

First Edition

Printed Edition ISBN: 978-0-916727-98-7
ePub ISBN: 978-1-60940-231-0
Kindle ISBN: 978 1 60940 232-7
Library PDF ISBN: 978-1-60940-233-4

Wings Press
627 E. Guenther
San Antonio, Texas 78210
Phone/fax: (210) 271-7805

On-line catalogue and ordering:
www.wingspress.com
All Wings Press titles are distributed to the trade by
Independent Publishers Group
www.ipgbook.com

Library of Congress Cataloging-in-Publication Data:

Tafolla, Carmen, 1951-
  Rebozos : poems / by Carmen Tafolla ; paintings by Catalina Gárate García, with an
historical afterword by Héctor García Manzanedo. -- 1st ed.
      p. cm.
  Text in both English and Spanish.
  Includes bibliographical references.
  ISBN 978-0-916727-98-7 (alk. paper) -- ISBN 978-1-60940-231-0 (ePub eBook)
-- ISBN 978-1-60940-232-7 (Kindle eBook) -- ISBN 978-1-60940-233-4 (library pdf
eBook)
  1. Ekphrasis. I. Gárate de García, Catalina. II. García Manzanedo, Héctor, 1926- III.
Title.
  PS3570.A255R43 2012
  811'.6--dc23
                                    2012025730

Except for fair use in reviews and/or scholarly considerations, no portion of this book may
be reproduced in any form without the written permission of the author or the publisher.

To the unsung women in rebozos
and to those who have always carried on the strength
behind any nation
and every revolution

———◇———

Photograph by Agustín Victor Casasola, ca. 1915
Known both as "Soldaderas" and "Adelitas"
The Casasola Collection
Fototeca Nacional in Pachuca, Mexico

Contents

A Poet's Introduction

Carmen Tafolla, Ph.D.

El rebozo, the simple Mexican shawl, is that everyday item which we wrap around our lives like an emotion, an expression, an instrument. With it we carry our children or bury our dead. We cover our tears or dance out our joy. It is our hands, our face, a reflection of who we are.

In its threads are interwoven the elements of our lives—dreams, frustrations, hope, grief. Hidden in its drapes and folds are the longings and the loves of our hearts. More than a garment, more than an object, a rebozo is our history. And in its texture lies the pattern of our future.

The rebozo has become a symbol of our womanhood, connecting us across classes and across languages, weaving us together like threads in the larger rebozo of this world, relating us, campesina to artist, artist to poet, poet to dancer, dancer to reader, reader to campesina. We are all, in the end, working the same field of corn, carrying the same load of wood, midwifing with the same care our loved ones, through birth or through death. We suffer storms and solitude, loss and longing, the interminable waits, the inconsolable disasters, the unfathomable loves. But we are all, in the end, reclaimed into the warmth of the same earth, this earth whom we choose to see as una enrebozada, a Mexican woman draped most elegantly and most eloquently in her rebozo.

This book cannot be traced solely to the artist, the poet, and the dancer that co-created, weaving into and out of each other's expressions. The central work of art celebrated here is the rebozo itself and the many centuries of women on this continen—Indigenous, Mestiza, Criolla, Pre-Columbian, Colonial, Revolutionary, Modern Feminist—who used their rebozos as creative instruments in their lives. And that creative process, which had begun centuries before, was repeated in the lives of these three women—Catalina, Rosa, and Carmen.

Catalina traveled through the rural regions of Mexico, her pencil and paper never too far from her grasp. She began to observe the women in the fields, to feel their emotion and their strength, and the way that was often expressed in the simplest of items—a jarro, a basket, a rebozo.

Catalina noticed the way the women draped their rebozos so gracefully across their shoulders, and then shifted them so adeptly to carry a baby at their breast or a load of wood across their backs. She watched them hour after hour, and she memorized the folds of their rebozos.

Catalina and Carmen . .
. . . caption . . .

Rosa scanned the eyes of the children, crushed by the prejudice and the oppression of the institutions that surrounded them. Rosa searched for a symbol, a vehicle with which to express the beauty she saw in her borderlands culture, a weapon with which to fight the depreciating messages and the vacuum that gripped the center where pride and sense of heritage should dwell.

Rosa picked up her rebozo and decided to dance with it. She danced to battle against discrimination and poverty, against stereotypes and shame, to dance and to teach, until people could see and understand the great wealth that lay woven into her culture on both sides of the border.

"It's because of Pancho Villa that I am here in the United States. My grandmother worked for Villa as a cook during the Revolution. When Villa's army landed in Juárez, my grandmother did too. It was there my mother was born. The fate that convinced my mother and father to cross a mile north in to El Paso, is the same fate that saw me born in this country and a citizen of the U.S."

Carmen went through the streets of her barrio, collecting the stories of the viejitas in their rebozos, trying to document the way each life, like each rebozo, seemed to unfold from a weaving of many threads. From the soldaderas who had immigrated after the Mexican Revolution to the descendents of the Spanish settlers of San Antonio two hundred years before to the great-grandchildren of the native Indians of this place by the river, they seemed to form a fabric of their own, weaving together many colors in one expressive statement. She heard the ancestors whispering over her shoulder, and the voices of the future sprouting forth. She picked up her pen and began to write.

Catalina was moved by the stories of her parents' generation, stories of women so poor but so courageous they would pack up their belongings in the folds of their rebozos and go into battle, leaving everything behind but their love and their courage. She had known the daughters of these women, as she worked in the fields in anthropological research—women who had little or no opportunities, but whose character could hold them up even as the walls of their worlds collapsed around them. Catalina picked up her brush and began to paint.

Catalina pulled the large canvases out from the closet in her studio. "This is what I'm working on now," she told Carmen. "I wanted you to see them because I feel we are both in parallel threads, going deep within our roots as women, as Mexicanas, to find that which is most universally human."

The book was called *Sonnets to Human Beings*, because Carmen said the time had passed when we could afford to write sonnets to "just one beloved." It is time to write sonnets to the whole human race. The German publisher intended to publish it on October 12, 1992, the 500th anniversary of the arrival of Columbus to American shores, but while the manuscript was being translated into German, Ernie Padilla at Lalo Press accepted it for a critical edition to be published months before the German one. The manuscript was ready but the question of cover art remained. "I want you to look at this series of women in rebozos by Catalina Gárate," Carmen told her editor. "That's what I want on the front cover of my book. That's what will speak the voice I want to speak – simple, but powerful. Unashamedly authentic to its roots, but universal."

"Carmen!" sighed Sally, eyes wide with amazement, fingers caressing the front cover of the book. "Who is this artist? This is beautiful. She's awakening but she's also spreading her wings, like a butterfly, a dawning, a metamorphosis."

It had been two years since the book had been published, but still Carmen could not pick up the volume without staring at the cover. "Who are you?" she finally asked the woman in the red rebozo, "And why are you still haunting me?"

Then the woman answered, and Carmen picked up her pen to record the answer. Flying home, tired from a performance, she was ready to close her eyes and rest, but the woman was speaking, and the plane, the clouds, the other passengers disappeared. The red rebozo was transformed into wings, and they carried her into a poem.

"Cata!" whispered Carmen into the telephone, "She's talking to me! Why is she so alive? Why are they ALL so alive? Each of these rebozos speaks!"

"That's what I wanted," Catalina confessed, "To let each painting speak only one single emotion —to let it be expressed in the colors, in the woman's stance, but especially in the rebozo, the rebozo that carried that woman's secrets, her pain, her desires, and her power too."

Later that evening, again long distance, Carmen read Sally the newly crafted poem.

"You're right, Carmen, she is alive. But you say there are other rebozo paintings too? Do you think Cata might let us exhibit them here?"

The series had included ten women. They had been stored in Cata's studio closet. But now, the rebozos' voices had whispered among the women, had grown to a murmur, a hum, and finally a voice that demanded its flight. Sally spoke to Florence, Pilar to Rosa, Catalina to Carmen, Carmen to Martha, and all the women in their rebozos pointed their heads and rolled their brows until Catalina turned to see the other five women, clad in rebozos, standing in her studio.

And she began to paint again. This time the whispers of the women called for their missing companions until they were all done.

Catalina stared at those fifteen rebozo-clad women who surrounded her in her studio. Each one of them had something to say: hope, fear, love, loneliness, longing… She took the brush again and signed each of the new paintings with assertive strokes: Gárate.

"Carmen," sighed Catalina, "Your poems speak voices from the same pueblos that birthed these rebozos. From two sides of the border, yours Chicanas and mine Mexicanas, they come from the same roots. You were writing in Texas of a curandera, and I was painting a curandera in California. You write of the Indian woman's nine month wait for the baby, I paint the Indian woman, nine months pregnant in la Espera. I paint the candle of a mourner in La Ofrenda, you write the voice of the mourner in We Never Die. People should see this art and these poems together."

"She's right" said Sally, "I want to exhibit her art with your poetry. And I want to exhibit them in El Paso."

"But Sally" Carmen protested, "many of these paintings speak emotions for which I have no poem."

"You could write them," whispered Sally.

So the poems were written, one voice per portrait, some in English, some in Spanish, while Carmen insisted they did not come from her. They had come from fifteen women—these women in the rebozos.

Rosa had not yet seen Catalina's paintings. All she had seen was a poem, about a woman in a red rebozo spreading her wings. Rosa had worked with generations of artists, dancers, cultural workers. She had taught the children and the grandchildren of her students and had always emphasized the message, "Be who you are. Be proud of who you are." Rosa read the poem of the Rebozo Rojo and shouted out, "I want to dance this! I want to tell them they can bloom like flowers, like a dawn, like the someone beautiful they are."

On February 8, 1996, at the University of Texas El Paso's Centennial Museum, the poetry and art exhibit "Rebozos y Voces" opened to an eager crowd of students, teachers, community leaders, and people from both sides of the border who just wanted to see their reflections in the faces of their grandmothers, mothers and aunts. Catalina Gárate, Carmen Tafolla, and Rosa Guerrero were there. Catalina Gárate had painted five oil paintings in two months. Carmen Tafolla had written ten original poems in nine days. Rosa Guerrero had choreographed the "Rebozo Rojo" dance in one week. Sally Andrade, Director of Institutional Planning, Research and Evaluation, Florence Schwein, Director of Centennial Museum, and Pilar Herrera, El Paso Collaborative for Academic Excellence, had brainstormed the funding, program, and publicity for the event. This entire creative tempest had occurred between October 1995 and January 1996.

The exhibit would go on to be seen in San José, McAllen, Corpus Christi, Fresno and Austin. The poems would go through several transformations in two languages, and a sixteenth portrait would join las hijas enrebozadas de Cata.

Cata, Carmen, Rosa, and centuries of women in the Americas join together to bring you this rebozo, woven from the threads of many lives and different disciplines, a tapestry of the experience of women on these American continents. And of women everywhere.

Introducción Poética

Carmen Tafolla, Ph.D.

El rebozo, esa sencilla chalina mexicana, es una prenda diaria con la que envolvemos nuestras vidas, es como una emoción, una expresión, un instrumento. Con él cargamos nuestros hijos o enterramos nuestros muertos. Con él cubrimos nuestras lágrimas o bailamos llenas de regocijo. Un rebozo es nuestra cara, son nuestras manos, es una reflexión sobre quiénes somos.

En sus hilos están entretejidos elementos de nuestra vida: sueños, frustraciones, esperanzas, pesares. Escondidos entre sus pliegues están los anhelos y amores del corazón. Más que una prenda, más que un objeto, el rebozo es nuestra historia. Y en su textura yace el diseño de nuestro futuro.

El rebozo se ha vuelto un símbolo de la mujer mexicana, el diseño haciendo conecciones por encima de idiomas y de clases sociales: trenzándonos juntas en un gran rebozo de este mundo, relacionándonos a una campesina con una artista, a una artista con una poeta, a una poeta con una bailarina, a una bailarina con una lectora, a una lectora con una campesina. Al fin y al cabo, todas estamos labrando el mismo campo de maíz, cargando el mismo pedazo de madera, haciendo de parteras a nuestros queridos, con el mismo cuidado a la hora de nacer que a la hora de la muerte. Sufrimos tormentas y soledades, pérdidas y anhelos, esperas interminables, desastres inconsolables, amores incomprensibles. Pero finalmente, todas estamos recogidas en la calidez de la misma tierra, esta tierra que entendemos como una enrebozada, una mujer mexicana cubierta de lo más elegante- y locuazmente en su rebozo.

Este libro no se puede atribuir únicamente a la pintora, a la poeta y a la bailarina que lo co-crearon, entrelazando expresiones internas y externas de cada una. La obra de arte central aquí es el rebozo mismo y siglos de mujeres en este continente –indígenas, mestizas, criollas, revolucionarias, feministas modernas—quienes usaron sus rebozos como instrumentos creativos en sus vidas. Y este proceso creativo, que ha empezado hace siglos, fue repetido en las vidas de estas tres mujeres – Catalina, Rosa y Carmen.

Catalina viajó a través de México rural, con su lápiz y papel siempre al alcance de la mano. Observó a las mujeres en los campos, sintió su emoción y su fuerza, y la manera en que se expresaban en los objetos más simples –una jarra, un cesto, un rebozo.

Catalina notó la gracia en que estas mujeres se ponían los rebozos sobre sus hombros y luego los acomodaban hábilmente, ya para cargar un bebé en su pecho, ya para cargar madera sobre la espalda. Las veía por horas y memorizó los pliegues de sus rebozos.

Rosa escudriñó los ojos de los niños aplastados por el prejuicio y la opresión de las instituciones que los rodeaban. Buscaba un símbolo, un vehículo que expresara la belleza que ella veía en su cultura de la zona fronteriza, un arma con la que combatiera el vacío y los mensajes desvalorizadores que controlaban el centro el cual deberían habitar el orgullo y el sentido de herencia.

Rosa tomó su rebozo y decidió bailar con él. Bailó para luchar contra la discriminación y la pobreza, contra estereotipos y contra la vergüenza, y decidió seguir bailando y enseñando, hasta que la gente pudiera ver y entender la gran riqueza plasmada en los tejidos de su cultura de ambos lados de la frontera.

"Fue por Pancho Villa que estoy aquí en Estados Unidos. Mi abuela trabajó para Villa como cocinera durante la Revolución. Cuando el ejército de Villa se asentó en Juárez, mi abuela hizo lo mismo. Allí fue donde nació mi madre. El destino que llevó a mi madre y a mi padre hacia el norte, a El Paso, es el mismo destino que me vio nacer a mí en este país, ciudadana de EEUU."

Carmen iba por las calles de su barrio recolectando historias de viejitas en sus rebozos, intentando documentar la manera en que cada vida, igual que cada rebozo, parecía desplegarse desde el tejido de tantos hilos. Desde las soldaderas, que habían inmigrado después de la Revolución Mexicana, a las descendientes de los colonos españoles en San Antonio doscientos años antes, a las bisnietas de los indios nativos de ese lugar a la orilla del río, todas ellas parecían formar una tela, tejiendo muchos colores en una sola declaración. Escuchó a sus ancestros susurrar por encima de su hombro y a las voces del futuro brotar. Tomó su pluma y empezó a escribir.

Catalina quedó conmovida por las historias de la generación de sus padres, historias de mujeres tan pobres pero tan valientes, dispuestas a empacar a sus pertenencias en los pliegues de sus rebozos e ir a las batallas, dejándolo atrás todo, menos su amor y su coraje. Ella había conocido a las hijas de esas mujeres ya que trabajaba en los campos en investigación antropológica – mujeres que han tenido pocas o ninguna oportunidad, pero cuyo carácter pudo mantenerlas arriba incluso cuando las paredes de sus mundos se colapsaban alrededor de ellas. Catalina tomó su pincel y empezó a pintar.

Catalina sacó del closet de su estudio varios lienzos grandes: "En esto estoy trabajando ahora", le dijo a Carmen. "Quería que los vieras porque siento que las dos seguimos hilos paralelos, yéndonos profundamente a nuestras raíces como mujeres, como mexicanas, para encontrar lo más universalmente humano."

El libro se llamaba *Sonetos a los Seres Humanos*, porque Carmen dijo que ya se habían acabado los tiempos cuando nos podíamos permitir escribir sonetos a un solo ser amado. Llegó el tiempo de escribir sonetos a toda la raza humana. Un editor alemán iba a publicarlos el 12 de octubre de 1992, el quinto centenario de la llegada de Cristóbal Colón a las costas americanas, pero mientras el manuscrito se estaba traduciendo al alemán, Ernie Padilla en Lalo Press lo aceptó para una edición crítica que se publicaría meses antes. El manuscrito estaba listo pero la cuestión de la portada quedaba pendiente. "Me gustarí a que vieras esta serie de mujeres en rebozo de Catalina Gárate", dijo Carmen a su editor. "Esto es lo que quiero en la portada de mi libro. Esto es lo que va a expresar la voz que yo quiero expresar – simple pero poderoso. Auténtico y sin vergüenza de sus raíces, y al mismo tiempo universal."

"¡Carmen!" exclamó Sally, con ojos muy abiertos por el asombro, los dedos acariciando la portada del libro. "¿Quién es esa artista? Es bellísimo. Esa mujer se está despertando pero también está estirando sus alas, como una mariposa, un amanecer, una metamorfosis."

Pasaron ya dos años desde cuando se había publicado el libro, pero Carmen aún no podía tomarlo en sus manos sin clavar los ojos en la portada. "¿Quién eres?" le preguntó finalmente a la mujer en el rebozo rojo, "¿y por qué me estás persiguiendo?"

Entonces la mujer le contestó y Carmen tomó su pluma para retener su respuesta. Estaba volando a casa, después de una presentación dramática que había presentado, lista para cerrar sus ojos y descansar, pero la mujer seguía hablando y el avión, las nubes, los otros pasajeros iban desapareciendo. El rebozo rojo se convirtió en alas y éstas la llevaban hacia el poema.

"¡Cata!" susurró Carmen en el teléfono, "¡ella me está hablando! ¿Por qué está tan viva? ¿Por qué TODAS ellas están tan vivas? ¡Cada uno de esos rebozos habla!"

"Eso es lo que yo quería," confesó Catalina, "que cada pintura expresara una sola emoción – que la dijera en colores, en la postura de la mujer, pero especialmente en el rebozo, el rebozo que carga sus secretos, su dolor, sus deseos y también su poder."

Esa misma noche, en otra llamada de larga distancia, Carmen le leyó a Sally el nuevo poema.

"Tienes razón, Carmen, ella está viva. ¿Pero dices que hay más pinturas de rebozos? ¿Crees que Cata nos dejaría exponerlas aquí?"

Rosa, Catalina and Carmen at the University of Texas at El Paso Centennial Museum, 1996.

La serie consistía en diez mujeres. Habían estado almacenadas en el estudio de Cata. Pero ahora las voces de los rebozos que estaban susurrando entre esas mujeres, se convirtieron en murmullo, en rumor y finalmente, en una voz que demandaba su vuelo. Sally habló a Florence, Pilar a Rosa, Catalina a Carmen, Carmen a Martha, mientras las mujeres enrebozadas levantaban las cejas y señalaban con sus cabezas, hasta que Catalina por fin volteó a ver a las otras cinco mujeres paradas en su estudio.

Y ella empezó a pintar de nuevo. Los susurros en su estudio seguían llamando a las compañeras que faltaban hasta completar el número.

Catalina contemplaba a esas quince mujeres paradas en su estudio. Cada una tenía algo que decir: esperanza, miedo, amor, soledad, deseo… Tomó otra vez la brocha de nuevo y firmó cada una de las pinturas nuevas con una enérgica pincelada: Gárate.

"Carmen," suspiró Catalina, "tus poemas hablan con voces de los mismos pueblos que parieron a estos rebozos. De los dos lados de la frontera, tus chicanas y mis mexicanas vienen de las mismas raíces. Tú estabas escribiendo sobre una curandera en Texas, y yo estaba pintando a una en California. Tú escribes sobre la espera de nueve meses de una mujer india a su bebé y yo pinto a una embarazada de nueve meses en la Espera. Yo pinto la vela de una doliente en la Ofrenda, tú escribes la voz de una doliente en Nunca Moriremos. La gente debería ver mis pinturas al lado de tus poemas.

"Ella tiene razón" dijo Sally, "quiero exponer sus pinturas junto con tus poemas. Y las quiero exponer en El Paso."

"Pero Sally", protestó Carmen, "muchas de esas pinturas hablan de emociones para las que no tengo poemas."

"Los podrías escribir, "murmuró Sally.

De modo que se escribieron los poemas, una voz por cada retrato, unas salieron en inglés, otras en español, mientras Carmen insistía en que esos poemas no venían de ella. Venían de las quince mujeres – aquellas mujeres en rebozo.

Para entonces, Rosa aún no había visto las pinturas. Lo único que había visto era el poema sobre la mujer en rebozo rojo extendiendo sus alas. Rosa había trabajado con generaciones de artistas, bailarines, trabajadores sociales. Había enseñado a los hijos y nietos de sus estudiantes y siempre estaba enfatizando el mismo mensaje: "Sé quién eres. Sé orgulloso de quién eres." Rosa leyó el poema de El Rebozo Rojo y exclamó: "¡Yo lo quiero bailar! Yo les quiero decir que pueden abrirse como flores, como un amanecer, como algo bellísimo. Lo son."

El 8 de Febrero de 1996, en el Centennial Museum de la Universidad de Texas en El Paso, la exposición poética y pictórica "Rebozos y Voces" fue abierta a la ansiosa multitud de estudiantes, maestros, líderes comunitarios, y la gente de ambos lados de la frontera que buscaban ver su reflejo en las emociones y las caras de sus abuelas, madres y tías. Catalina Gárate, Carmen Tafolla y Rosa Guerrero estaban allí. Catalina Gárate pintó cinco óleos en dos meses. Carmen Tafolla escribió diez poemas originales en nueve días. Rosa Guerrero preparó la coreografía de la danza "Rebozo Rojo" en una semana. Sally Andrade, directora de la Planeación, Investigación y Evaluación Institucional, Florence Schwein, directora del Museo del Centenario, y Pilar Herrera, colaboradora para Excelencia Académica en El Paso, se la ingeniaron para conseguir los fondos, el programa y la publicidad para ese evento. Toda esa tempestad creativa ocurrió entre el octubre 1995 y enero 1996.

La exposición viajó para ser vista en Corpus Christi, Fresno, McAllen, Austin y San José. Los poemas pasaron por varias transformaciones en ambos idiomas y un décimo sexto retrato amplió las filas de las hijas enrebozadas de Cata.

Cata, Carmen, Rosa y siglos de mujeres en las Américas nos hemos unido para traerle a usted este rebozo, tejido de hilos de muchas vidas y diferentes disciplinas, un tapiz de experiencia de mujeres de estos continentes americanos. Y de dondequiera.

Rebozos

It is love that pulls the victory of my grandmother's rebozo from the Mexican Revolution and makes it dance, and me to dance with it.

—Rosa Guerrero

Mujeres del Rebozo Rojo

Who are we
las mujeres del rebozo rojo
who are always waiting for the light
hungry for the pink drops of morning
on the night's sky
searching for the sparkle of creation
of beginning
of life
on the dawn's edge
trying so hard
to open our eyes

Who are we
las mujeres del rebozo rojo
who want to reach and stretch and spread
and grow beyond our limits
yawning
pulling up our heads
pushing out our lungs
arching out our arms
resting only when in growth
transition
transformation
wanting only to be and
to become

to unfold our lives as if they were
rebozos
  revealing
    our inner colors
      the richness of our texture
        the strength of our weave
          the history of our making
  opening to
    all our fullness
      blossoms set free
spreading our wings to the reach of the sky
  and awakening
    to who
      we really
        are

Las Mujeres del Rebozo Rojo

¿Quiénes somos,
las mujeres del rebozo rojo?
las que esperamos siempre luz
hambrientas de las gotas rosadas,
del rocío matutino,
buscando en la noche
el destello de la creación,
de un comienzo,
de la vida,
al borde del amanecer,
haciendo lo imposible
para abrir los ojos.

¿Quiénes somos,
las mujeres del rebozo rojo?
Las que deseamos estirarnos
extendernos
expandirnos
y crecer más allá de nuestros límites
Despertar, levantar la cabeza,
llenar los pulmones, arquear los brazos,
y descansar solo en crecer
en transitar
en transformarnos
con el deseo único de ser
y llegar a ser

Desplegar nuestras vidas como si fueran
rebozos
    revelando sus colores internos
    la riqueza de nuestra textura
    la fortaleza de la urdimbre
    la historia de nuestra creación

  Florecer
en todo nuestro esplendor,
capullos abiertos
Extender alas hasta el borde del cielo

Y despertar
    a quienes
      realmente
        somos

Rebozo Rojo
(Oil on canvas)

This painting of a woman awakening to the dawn was chosen as the front cover for one of Tafolla's poetry collections, and later became the inspiration for the creation of this art and ekphrastic poetry book by Gárate and Tafolla.

They Call Me Soledad

Soledad
lives inside me
lives where the rebozo
wraps around my heart
where the work that's mine
is mine alone

where the questions
have no answers
and I alone
must answer them

Soledad
lives inside me
where the face unpainted
lives without a face
and only light
can wash it

where the desert and the mountains meet
and I alone must greet them
must wait to take their dawn
their icy breath, their searing heat

Soledad
lives inside me
carries my face
carries my name
but even when her name is called
only I can answer for her
so I take what life has handed me
squeeze from it
the sweetness of the cactus juice
the warmth of sunlight free upon my face
the deep, rich strength of one who answers
to the name of
Soledad

Me Llamo Soledad

Soledad
vive dentro de mí
vive donde el rebozo envuelve
mi corazón

Donde las preguntas
no tienen respuestas
y sólo estoy yo
para contestarlas

Soledad
vive dentro de mí
en un vacío
al parecer sin cara
que sólo la luz
anima y lava

Donde el cielo y la tierra
se encuentran
y sólo estoy yo
en esa vastedad
de intenso colorido
de contrastes
de calor y hielo

Soledad
vive dentro de mí
tratando de borrar mi nombre
de borrar mi cara
Pero yo sé como
exprimirle
el dulce jugo a la tuna
gozar
del calor del sol
acariciando mi cara
y sentir adentro
la rica fuerza
de quien puede responder
al nombre de
Soledad

Soledad
(Oil on canvas)

Many young women who work as criadas, child-maids turned over to a household as young as eight or nine years old, often work, clean house, cook and raise the children for a family their entire lives. With no one to turn to but their employers, many of these young women find their resilience and their maturity within their own internal strength. Soledad, a common name for women in Mexico, means Solitude.

La Witch

Watch out for La Bruuuuja, La Witch
I saw her last night, wrapped in silence
wrapped in her magic and potions for love
wrapped in things that confuse the sky up above
Steaming brews, yellow powders, dried leaves
Strange butterflies always around her
of odd, unnamed colors and, by her head,
hummingbirds green with rainbow-dust wings
She looked at the heavens and stars appeared!
She looked at the wind and it started to howl!
And then she almost looked at me
A look with no face and
instead of eyes
Two deep mysteries
full of possibilities
full of sighs

full of vision into the heart
full of
powers
which I
will
request
to enchant and
entrance
the One I watch
the One I want
the One who will be
mi amor

La Bruja

Cuida'o con la bruja
que anoche la vi
envuelta en silencio
en magias y amores
que al cielo confundan
Pociones amarillentas
Brebajes hirviendo
Hojas secas, extrañas flores
Mariposas pequeñas de raro color
y siempre cerca de su cabeza
colibríes verdes
con pechitos rojos
y alas irisadas

Miró al cielo
y salieron estrellas
Miró al viento
y comenzó a soplar
Y casi volteó hacia mí
Una mirada sin cara
y en vez de ojos
misterios profundos
poderes
que iré a pedir
para conseguir
a ese
al que quiero
a mi amor

La Bruja
(Oil on canvas)

"The woman with powers
was often feared, but she
also became a resource
when powerful or even
magical intervention was
required. Brujas were also
sought out to cure mal de
amores, using humming-
birds as amulets for love."
—C.G.

Waiting

Time is an animal
I do not understand
A young coyote
too shy
to come
too near
I whisper
offer morsels sabrositos
open hands, blooms of hope
but he stays just outside
my reach

Lungs sigh
crawl through hours of dry adobe dust
I try to coo him into creeping close
but gold coyote eyes twitch restlessly
flash their untamed distance

Listen, timid one
I breathe quietly
hands still as stones,
Coyotito,
rebozo silent as the desert's breath
I'll even turn my head away
promise not to lift my gaze
if only you will come
near enough
to touch

La Espera

El tiempo es un animal
que no entiendo,
un coyotito muy tímido
que no se me quiere
acercar
Le ruego
ofrezco antojitos sabrosos
manos llenas, capullos de esperanza
pero huraño
lejos de mi alcance
se queda

Pulmones sin aire se arrastran
por las horas de polvo seco
Trato de acurrucarlo
acercarlo hacia mí
pero esos ojos dorados de coyote
relampaguean su indomable distancia

Oye, tímido,
te prometo respirar quedito
mis manos tranquilas como piedras,
coyotito,
mi rebozo tan silencioso
como el susurro del desierto
Te prometo voltear la cabeza
no levantar la mirada
si tan solo te acercaras
y te dejaras
tocar

La Espera
(Oil on canvas)

"Interminable waits create
their own emotions. This is
a painting of paralelismo
between the patient waiting
for the birth of a child and
the mother waiting for the
birth of a child." —C.G.

To Juan

When the Revolution came
my world didn't fall apart
My world doesn't fall apart for
a revolution
You
are my revolution, Juan

When I left home
my world didn't fall apart
because we make a home anywhere, Juan,
in the open air, under this roof of stars
I can make do
with almost nothing
My rebozo - a bed
My breast - your pillow
I have corn to make you tortillas
and even a little bag of sávila
and hierbitas to heal your wounds
I don't need much
Just one
thing
Don't you die on me, Juan,
because then
my world
would
come apart

Even now
I feel the walls
caving in on me
coming down on me
crumbling
collapsing
in this house we've made
of sky, of blood,
of *Revolución*.

A mi Juan

Cuando vino la Revolución
no se me cayó'l mundo
Mi mundo no se cae por revolución
Mi revolución eres tú

 Cuando me fuí de la casa
no se me cayó'l mundo
Qui'al cabo aquí hacemos casa, Juan
a pleno cielo raso
Aquí traigo mi petate
mi metate
y el perico
Aquí te tengo tus tortillas
Aquí en mi pecho tu almohada
Hasta la sávila en el morral, pa' las heridas
No nec'ito mucho yo
Nomás
No te me mueras, Juan
qui'a'i sí se me cae el mundo

Ahora mesmo
Se me están derrumbando las paderes
de esta casa hecha de cielo, sangre,
y Revolución.

Soldadera:
Homenaje a
Casasola
(Oil on canvas)

An homage to one of Agustín Victor Casasola's many iconic photographs of soldaderas, women who joined the Mexican Revolution on the battlefronts. Gárate states, "For me, Casasola's foto represents the epitome of the soldadera's participation in the Revolution. But while her face, even with its anguish and anxiety, is beautiful, my soldadera is horrorosa, the other side of the coin, with all the loyalty of a chaotic, embattled and bloody time, which she did not understand but whose walls she felt collapsing in on her."
The title of the Spanish poem here "A Mi Juan" reflects the revolutionary corrido, "La Rielera".

Clearing the Path

All You Hulking Bad Spirits
        Go Away
All You Icy Black Shadows
        Go Away
YOU and YOU and YOU, Evil Winds
        Go Away
Make Way

The tender body
of one of our own
is coming Home

Sweet Sunshine
        Warm the earth to hold him
Cool Rain of morning
        Wet his tongue
Blessed Smoke of mesquite and copal
        Clear him a Path

The tender body
of one of our own
is coming Home

Fire
        Burn all that is evil
Smoke
        Cleanse all that is soiled
Souls
        Kiss the eyelids of the cold one

For the tender body
of one of our own
One most loved
is coming home
One most loved
is coming
Home

Limpiando el Camino

Aléjate, espíritu malo
Aléjate, obscuridad
Aléjate, aire de maldad
que regresa a casa
el cuerpo de uno
de los nuestros

Hazle lugar
sol que calientas la tierra
Refresca su lengua
lluvia fresca de la mañana
Límpiale el camino
humo bendito, copal oloroso
que regresa a casa
el cuerpo de uno
de los nuestros

Quema, fuego
todo lo sucio
Limpia, humo
todo lo feo
Besa, alma
los ojos del frío
que regresa a casa
el cuerpo
del más querido
el cuerpo
del más
querido

Limpiando el Sendero
(Oil on canvas)

"In many rural areas, indigenous customs call for clearing the path of bad spirits with incense and copal smoke, especially in the face of difficulties or death. At one small pueblo several coffins arrived of indocumentados, young boys from Michoacan whom La Migra had tried to arrest. The driver had driven off in a panic, striking and killing them. The people were walking beside the coffins of these boys, and way ahead of them, all alone, was an elderly woman chanting prayers and spreading incense to clean the path."
—C. G.

Brown Seed

Sweet soft furrow of earthen power
crumbling with readiness, home of hope
nest as warm as sun's caress

Take this gift I toss you now
of prayered, well-saved brown seed
brown as you, brown as my calloused feet

that feel your promise like a kiss
a whisper that your patient breast
will feed this seed and feed me too

Perhaps I might then feed
another tiny seed
one whose eyes will open fresh

and earth-nest brown
the color of
my love

Color Café

color café esta semilla
que arrojo a la tierna tierra arada
color café la tierra
que lo abraza pa' que crezca
color café mis pies
que van por esta senda
de esperanzas
dando vida
tierra a semilla
semilla a mí
y yo—
a otra semillita
muy chiquita
que entre meses nacerá
abriendo ojos
que también serán
color café

La Siembra
(Oil on canvas)

"The connectedness of
the earth, of her feet, of
the seed she plants. . . "
—C.G.

Deep Inside the Storm

How COULD you?!
YOU, Tormenta! ¡Tempestad Fregada!
Your lightning fangs drip chaos
You flash your teeth and howl
Crack my world   Break my sky
Crush my tender sweet-birthed dreams
like flattened blooms beneath your hooves
You ruin everything
and then you ruin
more

You have no right!
Each thin word I shout
melts in your purple gusts
Your cruel teeth tear my ripest plans
devoured, destroyed down your dark throat
till nothing's left
not voice
not hope

But low and faint
between your screech and screams
my feet begin to pound
a drumbeat dance
a song of sun's return
on brown earth firm
My legs and arms grow fierce
some sunrise bloom of strength
insists with breathless pace
that my voice will once more be
found

Hear it now—a whisper grows
A rumbled power that will not stop
Hear it! Roaring, yes, from somewhere deep
inside your storm.

Muy Dentro de la Tempestad

¡Cómo PUDISTE!

¡TU, Tormenta! Fiera negra!
tus relámpagos colmillos
rompen el cielo, despedazan el mundo
Mis tiernos sueños
flores pisoteadas bajo tus cascos
Lo arruinas todo
y después arruinas
más

¡No tienes derecho!
Esas palabras flacas que clamo
se derriten en tus ráfagas moradas
Tus dientes crueles
los muerden, tragan, destruyen
Desaparecen en tu garganta oscura—
hasta que no queda
nada
ni voz
ni
esperanza

Pero entre los gritos y gruñidos
de la rugiente tempestad
resuena ya el ritmo
de mis pies firmes sobre la tierra
cantando el regreso de la luz
Las piernas furiosas cobran fuerza
Los brazos florecen cual el alba del poder
El susurro crece incesante—
Mi voz
Ya sé que sonará
desde acá muy dentro
dentro
de tu tempestad

Tempestad
(Oil on canvas)

"Even in a storm, the
rebozo serves a useful
purpose, an umbrella to
shield the woman from the
torrents of tempest. . . "
—C.G.

Curandera, Your Voice

like a low, mezquite breeze
whistles softly through half a lung
and crackles like dried leaves in ancient bottles
Patient teas, potent herbs stand ready
in dusty jars along your kitchen shelves
and in the crowded cabinets of your well-aged
mind, where remedios older than mountains
overlap histories with miracles
and labor with love

Your memory leaves not one space to waste
or out of grace, but leads the lemon rinds, comino
seeds,
reborn in dessicated age
as they grow to their purpose, stronger now
and ojos de venado add the haunting tenderness
of deer, the power of justice

Half-blind eyes whisper prayers through rippled
light
sift sunshine through the sounds of centuries
Shuffling slippers pause
Barking dogs bow quiet for this Mass

Aglow with blessing
your hands exceed
the boundaries of their bones
and reach
to make
the cure

Tu Voz, Curandera

como una brisa
de mezquite seco
Tus manos sabi-siglos
guían los tecitos y remedios
Las hierbas secas
cáscara de limón
semilla de comino
renacidas, fuerza nueva
marchan a su misión
Ojo de venado
reflejo del venado tierno
insiste en el
poder de la justicia

Curandera
arrastras tus viejas chanclas
por los portales de mis venas
bajas los botes de tu sabiduría
del gabinete de mi cabeza
En tus ollitas hierven ya
las hojas de mis sueños
Tus ojos rezan
filtrando la luz de siglos
Los perros, reverentes,
paran de ladrar

Con rayos del calor de sanar
tus manos sobrepasan
los límites de sus huesos
extiendes la mano
y
curas

Curandera
(Oil on canvas)

"The healing science of the
curandera goes beyond the
mere physical sciences. It
crosses the lines between
mental health, physical
health, spiritual health,
and the health of the entire
community. It requires
the healer to know the
individual, their culture, the
centuries of history behind
them, and the loving energy
that exceeds the physical
borders of our being."
—C.T.

Hidden Coves

Look inward
Let your eyes grow drowsy with life
Let thought carry you like a ship
floating slowly on those waves
of trembling candle light
until you find the shore
where you lay breathless
off the darkest hidden coves
of your soul

till you see Them
dark profiles staring
along the caverns' shore
Dreams Undreamed
and Sighs Unsighed
Hopes Long Vanished
and Ironbound Promises Kept
Treasures Cherished
and Things Lost
Somewhere Long Ago
stand side by side
observing you

while your ship floats by
searching the shores
scanning the most hidden
coves
of your soul
the candle still
flickering

Introspección

Ve hacia dentro
Deja que tus ojos se emborrachen de vida
y que el pensamiento te lleve como un barco
flotando en esas olas de luz de vela
hasta llegar a lo recóndito
de tu alma

Hasta que Los veas
En perfiles oscuros
Viéndote con miradas fijas
a la orilla de las cavernas
Sueños no Soñados
Suspiros casi Suspirados
Esperanzas Idas
y Promesas Cumplidas
Joyas Valiosas y Cosas Perdidas
Parados lado a lado
observándote

Mientras flota tu barco
buscando ensenadas
revisando lo más recóndito del alma
Mientras todavía tiemblan
las llamas

Introspección
(Oil on canvas)

How much lies inside
each one of us—stored,
forgotten, hidden, never
explored, never attempt-
ed, or. . . valued, deeply
experienced, cherished?

These Tacos

There is a place
where corn is ground by daily arms...
There is a place
where the stone comal warms gifts
from gardens that are asked
and each plate is prepared
and carved to fit the tastes
for that one mouth
whose sounds are known so well....
    - (from hay un lugar,
    Sonnets to Human Beings, 1992)

These taquitos
I made for you
for your mouth
whose taste I know so well
I know your belly too
and your hungers
your sighs and your desires
the rhythm of your chest
the softness of your breath
the way you burn me with your gaze
fill me with the heat of your skin
Your eyes half-closed, my lips half-open,
my shivering spine, your hands,
my moans, your
mouth
whose taste
I know so well

In these taquitos, the meat
is chopped small
and soft
for that missing tooth of yours
They're stuffed with tomatoes
sprinkled with cilantro
covered with chile that bites.
Un besito de sal
lemon drizzled like summer rain
and always add plenty of beans.
These taquitos
I made for you
for your mouth
whose taste
I know
so well

Los Taquitos

Los taquitos que traigo
los hice para tí
Pa' tu boca
que yo conozco muy bien
tu panza también
y tus hambres
tus anhelos y tus pasiones
el ritmo de tu pecho
lo suave de tu respiro
el modo en que me quemas
con tu mirada
la forma en que me llenas
con el calor de tu piel
Tus ojos medio-cerrados,
mis labios medio-abiertos,
escalofrío en la espalda, tus manos,
mi suspirar, tu
boca
que yo conozco
muy bien

Estos taquitos traen la carne
bien picada, pal diente que te falta
Llenos de tomate
salpicados con cilantro
lloviznados con chilito picante
un besito de sal
un chorrito de limón
¡y échale frijol a todo!
Los taquitos que traigo
los hice para tí
Pa' tu boca
que yo conozco
muy
bien

El Almuerzo
(Oil on canvas)

"Her basket of taquitos
still warm, this woman
waits for her compañero
to take a lunch break.
Her mirada speaks love,
loyalty, passion, the care
she took to pack this
lunch. . . " —C.T.

The Other Side of Tired

Traveler, there is no road.
You create the road by walking.
—Antonio Machado

I'm on the other side
of tired
where feet fall heavily
on paths that do not quibble
the buckets sit stodgily
still needing to be carried
the fires hissing to be lit
the mouths crying to be fed
nothing ever stops
until the end
the overworked candle
at the last flicker
burning to the nub
The camino spreads long before me
demanding but telling nothing
As I trudge forward
my rebozo falls gently about me
without resistance
without waste
I do not wonder what to do
and my feet do not ask where to go
only how to lift the weight
of their own leaden bones
once more and once more
and once
more

Al Otro Lado del Cansancio

Caminante, no hay camino,
se hace camino al andar.
—Antonio Machado

Mis pies caen directos, pesados,
intentos en caminos que no alegan
Ya me pasé de cansancio
Esperan más tinas a cargar
más fuegos a lumbrar
más bocas a llenar
Nada para hasta el fin
La vela sobrepasada
en su último aletear
quemándose hasta el tocón
El camino queda largo por delante
exigiéndome todo,
contestándome nada
Mientras voy paso a paso
mi rebozo cae sobre mis hombros
tiernamente
sin resistencia
sin desperdicio
No me pregunto qué hacer
y mis pies no preguntan para dónde
nomás cómo
levantar el peso
de esos huesos de plomo
una y otra vez
y otra
y
otra

Rebozo Azul
(Oil on canvas)

Me dijo el artista: "Yo
conozco esa mujer. Yo la
he visto. Quizá la he
sentido, dentro de mí."

Longing

A blue sigh locked so far inside

I only hear it when my soul's alone

awash in thoughts tender as

the opening of newborn eyes

a longing so purple it beats with no sound

whispers with no voice

those things never meant to be

What I wanted What I wished So long ago

Far beyond horizon's purple ridge

it fades like one faint feather of dust

inside a cloud that floats beyond my reach

then disappears

still

a distant echo trickles back to me

A faint and purple rippling echo of

one

long

blue

sigh

Añoranza

Hay un suspiro encerrado
entre violeta y dorado
que solo escucho a veces
cuando mi alma está aislada

Existe en mi corazón
una añoranza azul
por las cosas que el destino
nunca quiso permitir
en el verde mar
de mis memorias
de lo que quise
lo que hubiera querido
lo que anhelé
hace tanto

Muy lejos queda
más allá del horizonte
de montañas purpurinas
como plumita de polvo
dentro de una nube que
se me aleja y
ahora se desvanece
en ilusorio espejismo

Pero
con el viento
vuelve a mí el eco
el eco morado
que tiembla y refleja
un largo
lejano
suspiro
azul

Añoranza
(Oil on canvas)

"Long ago, a Filipino friend who had married an American and settled in California came to see my paintings. When she came to this one, tears filled her eyes. "What is this one called?" When I told her it was Añoranza, she told me how in her last year of high school she and her boyfriend had decided to marry as soon as they graduated. Shortly before graduation, he, inexplicably, dropped dead. 'I love my husband, she said. And my children are wonderful. But sometimes, I wonder what would have happened, what would— what if. . .'" —C.G.

Going with You

So many times, *Comadre*,
we'd go places together
to the fields
to the kitchens
When I gave birth
you were there
And when the rains tried to steal your harvest
I was there
When you pulled a muscle
or that time I had the fever
That time, you even fed my kids,
  toasting *tortillas* on my *comal*
while you laid wet cloths
so gently on my burning head

Comadre, want to go with me to church?
Comadre, want to go with me to Ofelia's?
Comadre ....

Now you lie there, on your kitchen table
Candles flicker around you like stars.

What a shame that our comadre passed away,
they say.
We'll really miss her,
miss going places with her.

But I've got one place yet, Comadre
one place more to go with you
I'll go by foot
Behind a wooden box
Going with you still
this one last time
Just to keep you company,
Comadre.

Hasta la Tumba

Tantas veces, Comadre,
que juimos juntas -
o a la pisca
o al metate
Cuando di luz, a'i 'tabas
Y cuando te urgía la cosecha, a'i 'taba
Que si ne'sitabas quien te sobara
O yo ne'sitaba quien me cuidara la fiebre
Que esa vez, hasta me hiciste las tortillas
pa los chamacos
mientras me aliviabas con toallitas frescas
en el fuego en mi frente

–¿Comadrita, vas conmigo pa l'iglesia?
–¿Comadrita, vas conmigo acá' mi prima?
–¿Comadrita –

Ahora estás tendida en tu mesa
velas to'o alderedor, como estrellas

Qué lástima que se nos murió la comadre,
me dicen.
Qué falta nos va a hacer 'ora sin ella

Pero yo sí, Comadrita, todavía voy contigo
a un lugar más
Iré a pié
detrás de un ataúd
nomás pa' acompañarte
la última vez,
Comadre

Dolientes
(Oil on canvas)

"How to capture an
emptiness, the dark space
left after the death of
someone we loved—
and love still, inside
that vacuum in our
core as we grieve. . . "
—C.T.

Offering to the Dead

I bring to you this offering
because I know
you will never die
In each fresh pink dawn
you stretch across the sky
In each leaf-jewel drop of dew
you cool my waiting tongue
As breezes slip past
sun's hot sand
you kiss my toes
caress my hand
The juicy sweet orange
bursts in my mouth
with mischievous spray
as you tease and comfort
to refresh my day

You will never die
You shine your smiles
through the final rays of light
You wait till the very last
dying glimmer before the dark
to surprise me, re-appear
with the unconquered sparkle
of your laughter
that plays between the stars

You will never die
I light these candles
leave these oranges
whisper these words
into the altar of your ear
feel your stubborn warmth
in each fistful of dirt
I press around its seed
as you press seeds of life and hope as well
Full of heat, full of love
right beside me

Ofrenda

Te traigo esta ofrenda
porque sé que nunca morirás
que en toda alborada cobriza estarás
En las gotas joyas de rocío
que tocan mi lengua
y apagan mi sed
Con las brisas danzantes
en la cálida arena del sol
besas ligeramente
los dedos de mis pies
En el dulce jugo de la naranja
que explota traviesa en mi boca
te ríes, acaricias
y refrescas mi quehacer

Sé que nunca morirás
porque dejaste tus sonrisas
en los rayos de luz
que esperan el último estello
del anochecer
para esconderse y luego reaparecer
jugando, chispeando
en las estrellas hoyuelos del cielo

Sé que nunca morirás
Prendo estas velas
Dejo estas naranjas
Susurro estas palabras
en tu oído, mi altar
Siento tu calor cabezudo
en cada puñado de la tierra
que yo surco
Porque tu siembras semillitas
de vida y de esperanza
también
Con calor, con amor
aquí merito
a mi lado
hoy

Ofrenda
(Oil on canvas)

In many Mexican homes,
November 1st and 2nd
are the Days of the Dead.
Altars to a family's deceased
members are decorated with
candles, small gifts, "zem-
poalsuchitl" flowers, and
the favorite food and drink
of the deceased. Often,
the celebration occurs at
the cemetery, or at a home
altar elaborately prepared,
but always, the sharing and
communication between the
dead and the living goes on.

You Can Tell We're Related

You can tell we're related
I can see it in your thunder and your rumble
your voracious appetite for sweet newness, for bold beauty
the Esperanza flowers you weave into your hair
the red seeds you hang from your neck
the wanting, the dreaming, the power in your belly

You can see it in the way I'm always building something new
yearning for something more
changing the way things are
Guts aching to open waterfalls, tear down walls
plant trees in unexpected places
press saved cositas to my heart

I can see it in your bright dawning arms, wide with welcome
Sunrays clear as cornsilk slip an extra plate on the table
always room, always room
shield the shivering under your mantle, fold them into growth
In the crisp of autumn's chill, toast them at your hearthfire
celebrate breath, hierba buena, anise, maíz, canela, cycles

You can see it in the way I quiver, dream, want, grow
My hard-headed terquedad determined to stand strong, free
always building mountains from the crater of my center
erupting revolutions passions transformations
the solid rock of my core the same taste as your soil
I expand I discard I recycle
Everything.
As do you

You can tell we're related, Madre
I wrap the shroud around my dead
to warm them, care for them, memorize them
see them in each feature of the newborn's yawn
and know you will wrap me too, some sun-filled day,
envelop me in the sky blue rebozo
of your loving shroud
lay me in the terca soft brown earth
of your still-growing
changing
heart

Se Nos Nota que Somos Parientes

Yo lo veo en tus truenos y en tus retumbos
En tu apetito feroz para lo nuevo y dulce,
lo bello y valiente
En las flores de esperanza que acomodas en tu pelo
En las semillas rojas que te cuelgas en el cuello
En el querer, en el soñar, en el poder en tu vientre

Tu lo ves en mi modo de siempre crear algo nuevo
añorando algo más
cambiando las cosas de cómo estaban
Abro una cascada, rompo una pared
Siembro árboles donde no se esperan
Aprieto cositas guardadas al corazón

Yo lo veo en tus brazos de amanecer
abiertos en bienvenida
Rayos del sol transparentes como melena de mazorca
Pones otro plato en la mesa
siempre hay lugar, hay lugar
Proteges a los débiles bajo tu manto,
los recoges en crecimiento
En la brisa de otoño,
los dejas tostaditos frente a tu hoguera
Celebran aliento, hierba buena, anís, maíz, ciclos

Tu lo ves en la manera en cómo me estremezco,
sueño, deseo, crezco
Mi terquedad me empuja a ser fuerte y libre
siempre construyendo montañas del cráter en mi centro
eructando revoluciones pasiones transformaciones
la sólida piedra de mi núcleo saboreando
a lo mismo que tu tierra
Expando. Deshecho. Reciclo
Todo.
Igual que tú

Se nos nota que somos parientes, Madre
Yo envuelvo mis muertos en el sudario
los caliento, los cuido, los memorizo
los veo en cada facción del bostezo de un recién-nacido
Y sé que tú también me envolverás algún día
en el rebozo celeste de tu amoroso sudario
y en la suave tierra terca
de tu corazón color café
que todavía crece y todavía
se transforma

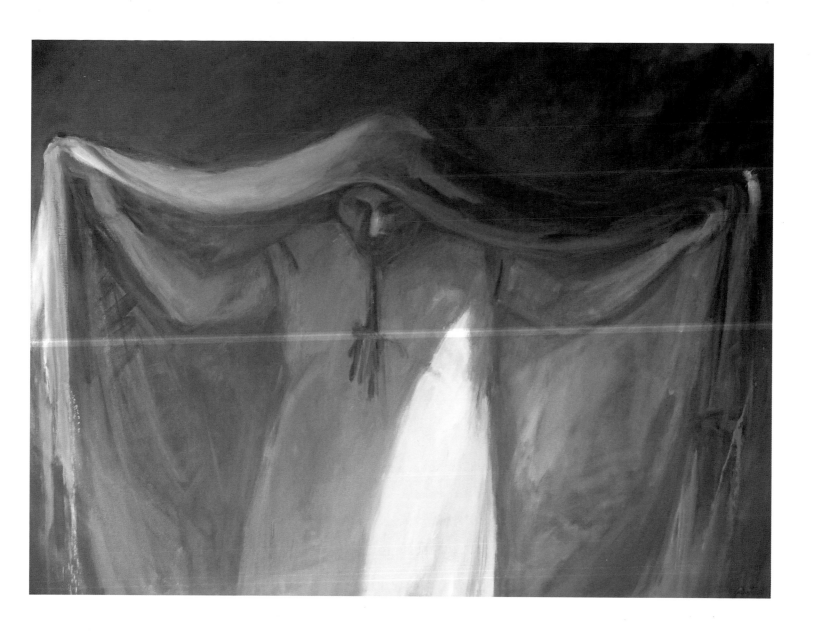

Madre Tierra
(Oil on canvas)

"My perception of the
rebozo is very close to my
perception of the earth
itself. It wraps and protects
us at birth, covering us as a
mantle of blue skies, and at
the end of our lives, opens
to receive us again." —C.G.

Artist's Statement

Catalina Gárate

The rebozo of a Mexican woman is more than a garment. In rural areas, the woman wearing a rebozo is invariably present, seeming to emerge from earth itself, as a symbol of strength and life. The rebozo seems to interweave itself throughout the entire life cycle of these women, a silent witness to their emotions, a tool to lighten the load of their everyday work. It can be used to cradle her newborn or to carry a child on her back. It can wipe away her tears, or hide her pain from public eyes. It can conceal, it can express. And at the end of her life, the rebozo may follow her still, becoming a shroud to wrap her body as it returns to the earth.

My purpose in this series has been to collect from my roots this unifying element, the rebozo, for it is a theme of profound significance to me. I see its interweaving role in the flow of life: birth and death, passion, hope, longing, poverty, loneliness, fear. . . But when I paint, I move beyond just a cultural experience, to reach feelings and emotions that are universal. To let the paintings speak, cry, survive.

The rebozo of a Mexican woman will always be for me, a symbol of her strength against the hardships of life, and a protective mantle that accompanies her throughout her existence.

Poet's Statement

Carmen Tafolla, Ph.D.

Gárate, haunted by the rural women of the campos and pueblos, the simple women solving the complex problems of life, love, and survival, painted into each color, and into the drape of each fold of the rebozo, the emotion and experience of that moment, of that life. Often in the paintings their faces are not visible; always, their rebozos are. Haunted then by Gárate's paintings and by the voices of the women of the barrios of Mexico and of the Southwesterrn U.S., I painted those colors into poetry, those expressions of posture and stance into voice.

The words of these women in the paintings are, like rebozos themselves, both soft and strong. Some are simple and direct, a prayer, a plea, a promise. The poetry lies in the courage of their lives. Others are more complex in their weaving, with more intricacy hidden in their folds. Together, they make the incredible fabric of women's voices. We are like threads together, blending and contrasting, till we create this nido of warmth, this comfort that is strength, this work of life "con su carga de amor sobre la espalda."*

———

* "Con su carga de amor sobre la espalda" from "Piropos al Rebozo" by Gregorio de Gante, in Poetas Mexicanos: Sus mejores poesías.

Afterword: The Rebozo as Cultural Icon

Hector García Manzanedo, Ph.D.

For over four centuries, the Mexican rebozo has been an important garment for women. Even in those regions of Mexico where modernization has occurred, women in rural and indigenous communities still wear their rebozos every day, not only to cover their shoulders or their heads, but also as a way to free their hands while carrying a baby on their backs, or to support a load of wood or fruit. The woman in a rebozo is an essential part of the image of Mexico, and as such has been depicted by artists such as José Agustín Arrieta, Edouard Pingret, and Saturnino Herran.

Although a daily part of the lives of Mexican Indians for the last 400 years, no written evidence has yet been found to indicate the rebozo's pre-Hispanic origin. While the first published mention of this garment by name dates to the Dominican friar Diego Durán in 1572, Vasco de Quiroga, Bishop of Michoácan from 1537 to 1565, had earlier issued ordinances for the religious order of Hospitalers, stipulating that women "should wear white cotton toques, with which to cover their heads and the rest of their bodies over the other garments they accustom to wear."[1] And the English merchant Henry Hawks noted in 1572 that indigenous women used to conceal themselves behind "a very fine shawl that shrouded them from the head to midway down the leg."

Viceroy Luis de Velasco established textile workshops in Texcoco in 1592.[2] The Royal Audience's regulations for the weavers did not apply to the Indians, "who are free to elaborate their artifacts without accounting to anyone, without restriction or impediment to their own ways of earning a livelihood."

Between 1603 and 1607, Ana Mejía, wife of Viceroy Juan de Mendoza y Luna, Marqués of Montesclaros, presented her chambermaid's daughter with a gift to mark her entrance into a convent, "a rebozo panel from Sultepec, white and blue," an item that was already one of the regulation garments for novices.[3] Sultepec, an Otomí village, had, by then, a well-established reputation for its textiles.

During the eighteenth century rebozos reached their peak of quality. The Royal Audience intervened in 1757 with precise specifications for their manufacture, signed by the Marqués de Cruillas. These ordinances laid down rules for size, weave, yarn type and designs. In 1794, the outgoing Viceroy, second count of Revillagigedo, left secret instructions to his successor the Marqués of Branciforte, explaining the rebozo: "This is an article of female attire, worn by all from the most elevated ladies to the lowliest wenches, and even by nuns." By 1796, it was the Marqués de Branciforte's turn to issue new regulations for rebozo making, imposing a particular twist of silk and cotton.[4]

Toward 1789, the city of Puebla boasted two hundred rebozo workshops, specializing in gold and taffeta. By the end of the eighteenth century, the rebozo had clearly become an indispensable garment and traditional art in Mexico.[5] This rectangle of cloth, woven with cotton, silk, or wool, with borders and fringes which are usually knotted to form geometric or animal figures, had become a symbol of the culture itself.

In the Morelia Archive, there is a 1768 mention of several old Salomonic rebozos, black with silver fringes: a fine Puebla example and another common one, a rebozo from the Sierra, a rebozo from the State of Mexico, one all silk item from Sultepec, and one ordinary piece from Ozumba.

In the State of Mexico there were also some famous pieces from Tenancingo, Tuxtepec, Xilotepec, Tejupilco and Calimaya. The latter village was famous for the refinement of its stitching. Also worthy of notice are Santa María del Rio in the state of San Luís Potosi, Zamora in Michoacán, Tulancingo, Acaxochitlán and Zimapán in Hidalgo, and Chilapa in Guerrero. Together these textiles conjure up a vanished age memorably evoked by José Agustín Arrieta, Edouard Pingret, Fanny Calderón de la Barca, and many others. But the skills that informed these marvelous rebozos have not been altogether lost. Nationally, ikat* remains the most admired form of decoration for rebozos.

At the beginning of the nineteenth century, the rebozo was indispensable for women of all social classes. "This garment was so popular that, during the First Empire (1832) the rebozo that la Güera (The Blonde) Rodríguez embroidered herself became famous; and in the Second Empire, Empress Carlota attended social functions wearing a rebozo." (Castello, 1989).

In those years in which the country searched, with profound patriotism, for its own sense of nationhood, the great popularity of rebozos among Mexican women of all levels of society increased the market for this garment.[6] Soon, rebozos produced by Indian weavers in their backstrap looms were insufficient to satisfy the demand, and faster, more efficient pedal looms were put into action. Even at present, it is possible to find both the mass-produced rebozos, and those woven on a backstrap loom side by side in market stalls in most regions of Mexico.

During the second decade of the nineteenth century, people from the recently established Mexican nation felt a need to create their own dress, to identify themselves with a national symbol. Due to the cultural diversity in the country, many indigenous styles of clothing existed, but none could serve to unify a newborn nation like the common denominator of a trans-group innovation, a dress that applied to merchant or servant, fieldworker or nun—the rebozo. In this way, the rebozo took on an important role in the life and the attire of Mexican women.[7] The rebozo was adopted and worn with pride and elegance by young and old, Indian and mestizo, rich and poor.

---

* The classic rebozo is made of cotton, silk or silk floss and its marbled pattern is achieved through ikat, an ancient technique that uses a tie-dying method. Actually the rebozos were made in specialized centers such as Tenancingo, State of Mexico; Santa Maria del Rio, San Luis Potosi; and other places of lesser importance such as Tejupilco, State of Mexico; Zamora and Tangancicuaro, Michoacan; Chilapa, Guerrero; and Moroleon, Guanajuato. They are sold in all Mexican markets, especially Ondian markets. It is important to note that almost all the places mentioned are found in regions with large indigenous populations. (Ruth Lechuga). At the beginning the cloth is narrow and oblong, formed by one single piece of cloth and stitched in two pieces, and is known as paño de embozo. The rapacejos are derived from the Spanish toca and the fringes are attributed to the influence of the Manila mantón. (Castello, 1989)

At the end of the war for independence from Spain in 1821, the new Mexican nation faced not only internal political strife, but also invasions from powerful European nations and even from the United States of America, to whom they lost almost one half of their national territory. For the rest of the nineteenth and much of the twentieth centuries, Mexicans were not spared from the suffering that wars and revolution bring, especially to the poor and the peasant populations. Mexican women often followed their men into battle, sometimes fought at their sides and, after the winners took the spoils of war, they returned quietly to their homes wrapped in their humble rebozos to cook, to bear children, and to toil in the fields next to their men to feed the family's meager existence.

From 1910 to almost 1923, Mexico was in the midst of a revolution which saw towns and families torn apart by political and ideological strife. Mexican women were involved from the beginning, although history too rarely has recognized their roles. Carmen Serdán fought, together with her mother and brothers, in one of the first attempts against the government in the city of Puebla; women strapped on guns and fought as soldaderas and as field officers; revolutionary women were recognized in folk songs, like the corridos La Valentina, La Rielera, Adelita, and others.[8] And when they died in the battlegrounds, their bodies were simply wrapped in their rebozos, and laid to rest where their blood had soaked the earth.

One of the best collections of photographs documenting the history of the Revolution of 1910 is that of Ignacio Fernández Casasola. The Casasola photographs capture the full depth of the emotions and the chaos connected with the Mexican Revolution. One photograph in particular depicts the fear, the hope and the desperation of the soldadera on the battlefield. From aboard the steps of a train, her mouth open in a shout, her eyes stretching to reach that which was left behind, her rebozo flying around her head, this soldadera represents the thousands of women who followed their men into the tornado that shook all of Mexico for more than a decade.

After the Revolution ended, peasants and factory workers alike returned to their homes and started the process of rebuilding their country. Corn and beans were planted in the fields, dust and decay were cleaned from the machinery, carbines and pistols were put away, and a new conscience started to emerge from the walls: José Clemente Orozco, Diego Rivera, David Alfaro Siqueiros, voices from this renewal of hope and justice, painted murals on public buildings depicting the dreams of the Mexican people. All three artists presented the peasant woman clad in a rebozo, either working or carrying flowers, toting guns or babies. And Mexican women saw themselves, and their part in history, reflected in those murals.

Why have rebozos engrained themselves in the fabric of the culture? Because they have multiple uses in the customs and way of the life of these women? Because the rebozo covers, protects and carries the newborn in its mother's arms, while leaving her hands free? Or because it lightens the load of peasant women who walk considerable distances with heavy burdens, first to carry wares to the market, and then to return home? It can be rolled and put on their heads to cushion a load, or to protect them from the heat of the sun. During the Mexican Revolution, women desperate to save their families' food from plunder stuffed ears of corn into the bosoms of their rebozos, often changing their figures substantially, but wrapping the rebozo tightly around them till their family's sustenance was assured.

Catalina, Hector, Rose and Carmen.

The rebozo became incorporated into the dance of Mexico as well, twirled above the head or wrapped around the shoulders; from the festivity of La Bamba to the solemnity of Zandunga, the rebozo became an integral part of the folkloric culture of Mexico. While modern urban areas of Mexico moved on to match the more European fashions of the era, in the provincias Indian and mestizo women continued to find the rebozo to be a central instrument in their lives, both practical and expressive. The outlying areas, from Central America to the Southwestern United States, also clung to this symbol of womanhood, elegant and simple, adaptable and strong.

The rumbling awareness of the search for roots became a dominant theme in the art of the U.S. Hispanic population, most publicly in the 1970s and 80s, but the voices of Latina women were not given a more focused reception till the late 80s and 90s. Writers, artists, and other professionals and community leaders raised their voices to be heard at the head of these who were struggling for recognition of their own uniqueness.

El Paso dancer and educator Rosa Guerrero explains her own response to the rebozos of Mexico this way: "As I see the rebozos, I see a little bit of Toluca, where my mother was born, a little bit of Aguascalientes, where my father was born, a little bit of Mexico City, where my grandmother died, and a little bit of Jalapa, Veracruz, where my grandfather is buried. In each rebozo, I see a little bit of womanhood and the struggles and survivals of the miracle of life, and of the women who were miracle workers."[9]

Through hundreds of years of Mexican history, the rebozo made its mark on each era. During the fight for independence from Spain in 1810, peasant women wore their rebozos with pride, to contrast with the Spanish and Creole women who dressed in the colorful and expensive Mantón de Manila, embroidered with silk from China and the Philippines. During the Revolution of 1910, soldaderas carried infants or guns, tortillas or bandages, courage and faith safe within the folds of their rebozos.

According to the artist Catalina Gárate, "The rebozo of a Mexican woman is more than a garment, and in rural areas, it could be considered an ethnic symbol which is present throughout her life cycle. The rebozo covers the rural woman in her everyday work; it helps to lighten the load, it can be used to cradle the newborn, and to carry her child on her back. It can wipe away her tears, or hide her pain from public eyes. It can conceal, it can express. And, at the end of her life, the rebozo may follow her still, becoming a shroud to wrap her body, as it returns to the earth… The rebozo of a Mexican woman will always be, for me, a symbol of her strength against the hardships of life, and a protective mantle that accompanies her throughout her existence."[10]

The dancer Rosa Guerrero concludes, at the end of an exhibit of Gárate's art and Carmen Tafolla's poetry: "We are stirring this all together, like cultural revolutionaries, for identity, stirring it como un mole, then weaving it, como un rebozo."[11]

Notes

1. Castello Itúrbide, Teresa. "Viceregal Rebozos," in *Rebozos de la Colección Robert Evers.* Mexico, Museo Franz Mayer, Artes de Mexico, pp. 52-53, n.d.
2. Ibid.
3. Ibid.
4. Ibid.
5. Ibid.
6. Lechuga, Ruth. "Indigenous Antecedents of the Rebozo," in *Rebozos de la Colección Rovert Everts.* Mexico: Museo Franz Mayer, Artes de Mexico, pp. 50-52. N.d.
7. Trejo Castro, Juan. *El Proceso de Cambio a Traves del Uso del Rebozo.* Casa de Tenancingo de Degollado, Estado de Mexico. Unpublished Thesis, Toluca, Mexico, 1993.
8. "Con su carga de amor sobre la espalda" from "Piropos al Rebozo" by Gregorio de Gante, in *Poetas Mexicanos: Sus mejores poesías.* Mexico: El Libro Español, 1957.
9. Interview with Rosa Gerrero. February 6, 1996, El Paso, Texas.
10. Gárate, Catalina. Artist's statement, "Rebozos y Voces" Exhibit, El Paso, Texas, February 6, 1996.
11. Op. cit., February 6, 1996.

Additional Resources

Armella de Aspe, Virginia, y Teresa Iturbide. *Rebozos y Sarapes de Mexico.* Mexico: GUTSA, 1986.

Bancen. *Santa María del Río, un Pueblo de Artesanos.* Mexico: Fondo de Cultura Bancen, 1990.

Castello Itúrbide, Teresa. *El Rebozo.* Mexico: Editorial GUTSA, 1989.

Durán, Fray Diego. *Historia de las Indias de la Nueva Espana, e Islas de Tierra Firme.* Mexico: Editorial Porrua, 1967.

Espejel, Carlos. *Las Artesanias Tradicionales de Mexico.* Mexico, SEP-Setentas, 1979.

Insituto de Investigaciones de la Universidad Autonoma del Estado de Mexico. *Catálogo de las Artesanías del Estado de México.* Mexico: U.A.E.M., 1962.

Lechuga D., Ruth. *La Indumentaria en el México Indígena.* Mexico: FONART-FONAPAS, 1982.

Marín de Paalen, Isabel. *Historia General del Arte Mexicano, Etno-Artesanias y Arte Popular.* Mexico: Secretaría de Educación Pública, Lecturas Mexicanas 108, 1988.

Nuñez y Domínguez, José de Jesús. *El Rebozo.* Mexico: Serie de Arte Popular y Folklore, Estado de Mexico. 1958.

Velázquez, G. Gustavo. *El Rebozo en el Estado de México.* Mexico: Biblioteca Enciclopédica del Estado de México, 1981.

Acknowledgments

This weaving of art and poetry, culture and universality, emotion and motion would have never happened if it had not been for the ánimo and apoyo of the following people. First of all, Dr. Hector Garcia, who cheered, appreciated, and encouraged Catalina's art for many long years, and finally ended up driving it in a U-Haul truck across the desert of the Southwest on TWO different and very long occasions, as he smiled and jokingly called himself, "Lolo el Treilero." Secondly, Dr. Ernesto M. Bernal, always an enthusiastic supporter of the arts and of women's creativity, who unfailingly encouraged my writing for the last 33 years, who listened carefully through every draft of this manuscript, and applauded at every reading. Gracias, mi amor.

And very especially, to Sally M. Andrade, who was the first person visionary enough to see Cata's art and my poetry and ask that they be displayed together, in a stunning exhibit at the University of Texas El Paso in 1996. Thank you, Sally, for having the gentle courage and extraordinary vision to my "But I don't have poems on some of the topics of her paintings" to respond, "You could write them..."

To Wings Press for courageously accepting a manuscript that five other presses had ignored.

To Rosa Guerrero, for weaving her rebozo dance throughout our Rebozo creation.

To Janka Klescova for translation of the introduction, and to Celina Marroquin and Janka Klescova for Spanish editing of the poems and for dancing the delicate balance between Spanish regionalisms and poetic eloquence. If readers note that the English and Spanish versions of these poems are more often than not different, it is because they were not translated, but I wrote each poem authentically in its own language, and insisted to my patient editors that each poem should have its freedom to be unique, even from its counterpart in the other language.

And to Norma Cantu, Bryce Milligan, and Barbara Brinson Curiel for suggestions and English editing; your ideas and reactions, and Antonia Castañeda's insistence on this manuscript speaking its own center have made all the difference.

All of you together have woven a rebozo to be cherished.

—Carmen Tafolla

On a personal level, I, as the artist, along with Dr. Carmen Tafolla as the poet, owe a debt of gratitude to the several persons involved in the development. of this book. It was Dr. Tafolla who wrote a first poem inspired by one of my paintings entitled "Rebozo Rojo" which was used as a cover on one of her books. Dr. Sally M. Andrade encouraged her to keep writing poems for the rest of the paintings in the "Rebozos" series. Both of them were instrumental in opening the doors for my first formal exhibit in El Paso, Texas. I must also acknowledge Mrs. Florence M. Schwein, former Director of the Museum of the University of Texas, El Paso for the opportunity to present my art there. Lastly, but not least, my thanks go to Mr. Bryce Milligan of Wings Press and editor of this book. His persistence in getting me to publish my art has made this book possible.

—Catalina Gárate García

Contributors

Carmen Tafolla is a native of the West Side barrios of San Antonio, Texas, where her ancestors have lived since it was the Republic of Mexico and before. The author of more than twenty books, she is widely considered one of the madrinas of Chicana Literature.   Tafolla has performed her one-woman show "My Heart Speaks a Different Language" internationally, and her works have been published in English, Spanish, German and Bengali. Tafolla has received numerous literary honors, including the Américas Award, The Art of Peace Award, the Charlotte Zolotow, two Tomás Rivera Mexican-American Book Awards, two International Latino Book Awards and the San Antonio Women's Hall of Fame. She teaches at the University of Texas–San Antonio where she is Writer-in-Residence for Children's, Youth & Transformative Literature. In April 2012, Tafolla was named the first poet laureate of San Antonio, Texas. Her newest dramatic performance, "Rebozos!" is based on the poems in this book.

Catalina Gárate was born in Tampico, Mexico, and studied at numerous art schools, including the "La Esmeralda" of the Mexican Ministry of Education, and the Academia de San Carlos of the National University of Mexico (UNAM.) She completed a B.A. and an M.A. in Art and Design at San Jose State University in California. She conducted studies at the National School of Anthropology and History in Mexico City, and participated in anthropological research programs in rural indigenous communities in several regions of Mexico jointly with Hector Garcia, pioneering research for Estudios Experimentales en Salubridad. She presently resides in San Jose, California, where she is at work on a series of abstracts. Garate's works have been exhibited in San Jose, Fresno, Austin, McAllen, Corpus Christi, and El Paso.

Hector García Manzanedo was a noted anthropologist and a Professor of Sociology at San Jose State University for more than twenty years. A native of Mexico City, he was a museographer at the Museo Antropológico de México and worked many years in indigenous communities in Mexico before accepting a position at San Jose State University teaching Research Methods. With several publications to his credit, he was also a critical part of the conceptualization and development of this ¡Rebozos! art and poetry project until his death in 2003. His article "The Rebozo as Cultural Icon" was written specifically for this book shortly after the book was conceptualized.

Rosa Guerrero is an internationally acclaimed dancer, educator, and humanitarian. Born on the border between El Paso, Texas and Juarez, Mexico, she has earned the respect of educators and artists throughout the American continents for her work with youth in areas of cultural understanding and personal affirmation. Named to the Texas Women's Hall of Fame, Guerrero has had a school named in her honor and several generations of students who have been impacted by her inspiring dedication to humanity.

Wings Press was founded in 1975 by Joanie Whitebird and Joseph F. Lomax, both deceased, as "an informal association of artists and cultural mythologists dedicated to the preservation of the literature of the nation of Texas." Publisher, editor and designer since 1995, Bryce Milligan is honored to carry on and expand that mission to include the finest in American writing—meaning *all* of the Americas— without commercial considerations clouding the choice to publish or not to publish.

Wings Press attempts to produce multicultural books, ebooks, chapbooks, CDs, and broadsides that enlighten the human spirit and enliven the mind. Everyone ever associated with Wings has been or is a writer, and we know well that writing is a transformational art form capable of changing the world, primarily by allowing us to glimpse something of each other's souls. Good writing is innovative, insightful, and interesting. But most of all it is honest.

Likewise, Wings Press is committed to treating the planet itself as a partner. Thus the press uses as much recycled material as possible, from the paper on which the books are printed to the boxes in which they are shipped.

As Robert Dana wrote in *Against the Grain,* "Small press publishing is personal publishing. In essence, it's a matter of personal vision, personal taste and courage, and personal friendships." Welcome to our world.

Colophon

This first edition of *Rebozos*, by Carmen Tafolla and Catalina Gárate García, has been printed on non-acidic paper using environmentally friendly inks by Regent Publishing Services in Hong Kong. Titles have been set in Futura Light type, the text in Adobe Caslon type. All Wings Press books are produced by Bryce Milligan.

On-line catalogue and ordering:
www.wingspress.com

Wings Press titles are distributed
to the trade by the
Independent Publishers Group
www.ipgbook.com
and in Europe by
www.gazellebookservices.co.uk

Also available as an ebook.

Printed in China.